Seriously, Bitch?

Cocksucker

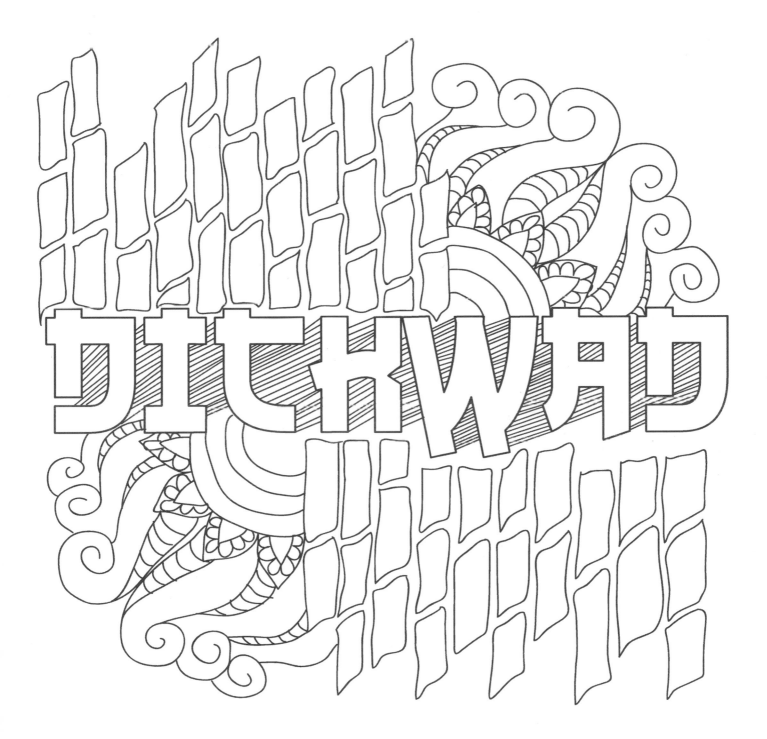

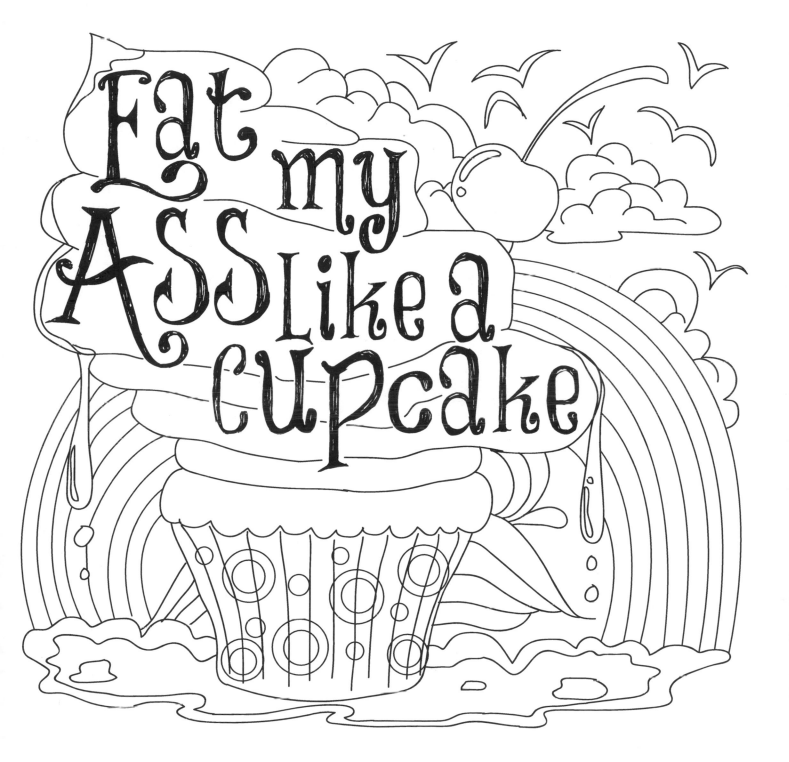

PRINT THIS BOOK

Download this entire book in printable PDF format at: colorfulswearing.com/GoFuckYourselfPDF

GET MY PREVIOUS BOOK FOR FREE

Every week, I send out new sweary coloring pages for free to all my e-mail sweary community. Join us now and instantly receive my entire last book in printable PDF format: colorfulswearing.com/freebook

CONNECT

I run a Facebook page where I share coloring pages, run contests and give you updates on my upcoming books. You can join me at: facebook.com/colorfulswearing

There is also an awesome private sweary Facebook group you can join, with artists and colorists from everywhere. We share free pages to color, run giveaways and contests. You can join the group here: facebook.com/groups/swearywords

And feel free to add me as a friend on Facebook. I enjoy sharing and connecting with all of you, artists and colorists alike, and I would be more than happy to connect with you too. You can add me here: facebook.com/alexfleming123

Would you be kind enough to review my book?

Reviews are my oxygen. Without your feedbacks, I would not be able to improve this book, nor would I be able to constantly make my new books better.

Reviews are also what make people buy my books.
In fact, you probably read some reviews before purchasing this one.

So if you enjoyed this book, please take 5 minutes to post an honest review on Amazon.
I would really, really appreciate.

With love,
Alex F.

Made in the USA
Lexington, KY
06 October 2017